About Time Too

Also by Peter Robinson

Poetry:

The Benefit Forms
Going Out to Vote
A Part of Rosemary Laxton
Overdrawn Account
Anaglypta
This Other Life
More About the Weather
Entertaining Fates
Leaf-viewing
Lost and Found
Via Sauro Variations
Anywhere You Like

Translations:

Six Poems by Ungaretti (with Marcus Perryman)
Selected Poems of Vittorio Sereni (with Marcus Perryman)
When I was at my Most Beautiful and other poems 1953–1982 by
Noriko Ibaragi (with Fumiko Horikawa)

Criticism:

In the Circumstances: about Poems and Poets

Editor:

With All the Views: Collected Poems of Adrian Stokes
Liverpool Accents: Seven Poets and a City
The Thing About Roy Fisher: Critical Studies (with John Kerrigan)
News for the Ear: A Homage to Roy Fisher (with Robert Sheppard)

PETER ROBINSON

About Time Too

'No answer from you yet – perhaps it is as well –
but do recollect – that all is at stake – the present
– the future – & even the colouring of the past…'
Lord Byron, 5 February 1816

CARCANET

Acknowledgements

I am grateful to the editors of the following print and electronic publications where the majority of these poems, or earlier versions of them, first appeared: *The Animist, Ariel, Bongos of the Lord, College Green, Cortland Review, English, fourW, London Quarterly, Meanjin, Metre, New Grains, New Observer, Notre Dame Review, Perihelion, Poetry Kanto, The Poetry Kit, PN Review, Prairie Schooner, Printed Matter, The Richmond Review, Salt, Samizdat, Shearsman, Stand Magazine, Swansea Review, Thumbscrew, The Times Literary Supplement*, and *Trout*.

Another version of 'Boundary Drive' appeared in Making Connections: *A Festschrift for Matt Simpson* (Stride, 1996). 'Playing Dead' was included in *News for the Ear: A Homage to Roy Fisher* (Stride, 2000).

Parts 1-7 and 23-5 of 'Via Sauro Variations' appeared in the *Notre Dame Review*; parts 9-20 were posted in *The Richmond Review*. The sequence was printed in a hand-bound limited edition by Julia Flanders at the Ridgeback Press, Providence, Rhode Island in 1999.

First published in 2001
by Carcanet Press Limited
4th Floor, Conavon Court
12-16 Blackfriars Street
Manchester M3 5BQ

The publisher acknowledges financial assistance
from the Arts Council of England

Set in 11/12pt Bembo by XL Publishing Services, Tiverton
Printed and bound in England by SRP Ltd, Exeter

Contents

ONE

Difficult Mornings

These mornings I'm not supposed to lie
late into the light or let you
wake from a dream and find it so
reassuringly warm, the curtains half-open,
a wisp of cloud above swaying pines;
there's barely time for last night's news
to stir me on this far side of the planet
with its aerial view of railway lines
running through a district in my home town
where a child's battered body had been found;
nor is it the moment now to gather
our strength up in a common end again
and then let one thing lead to another…
let alone click the alarm, have hours go by
following the grammar of a stubborn regret
in search of words that might mend or explain.

These mornings I'm not supposed to lie
snuggling under a duvet cover,
not supposed to be wondering whether
we can expect to have money enough
to last the rest of a life together;
no, pen in hand, I struggle to revise,
revise a voice into other people's prose
as if it were coaxing a weary lover
till the tongue as she's spoken put on a brave face
or exasperated, patience gone,
English itself were to sit up and tell us:
'Use me, yes, but use me well.'

Deceptive Landscape

Of all the happy accidents
to fall and dislocate a shoulder
slipping on the trodden ice
with a sudden wetness, cries
for help, and hospital we happened
to be wanting anyway...

Banked cumulus or snowy ranges
had shaded into sky, a whiteness
from which knife-edge strata
jutted like a Christmas
present and, overnight, changes
were promised us for later.

How snow, from a distance,
had deceived in broad daylight
this familiar wounded soldier
cradling his own mischance...
But you were not deceived
by dark glints, laden roof-lines

on the mountain road, descending,
for snow had played its part
already in that start of joy
at new life seen expanding
inside you, and sensed by
a hand strapped to the heart.

The Gift

for Mark Ford

Taking a short cut, we both noticed
bananas, pineapples, a bunch of grapes
abandoned on a bricked-up window sill.
'Yours,' you said, as we wandered past,
commanding me to use it –
as if more bits of orange peel,
and I the thrifty poet
strolling from café to restaurant.

There didn't seem anything in some fruit
left to rot where the back court turned
– except perhaps a mild taunt;
but you were the gift personified
and a friend I hadn't seen in years
with three-day beard, some mad ideas
about how to make a living. Life?
You were waiting for inspiration.

Only then among pictures seen, or unseen,
was Carlo Crivelli's *Annunciation*
(the one with, jutting from its frame,
a *trompe l'œil* apple and cucumber)
and in that distant afternoon
as no doubts started up from chance's
conjoining this and that, our time
folded back into its circumstances.

After Bansui

'And maps can really point to places
Where life is evil now:
Nanking…'

W. H. Auden

1

Steps climbed into bushes
at a turning as the road
chicaned through curtain walls;
a sign's arm pointed at rushes.

By hinge-posts, leaves and berries
papered over faults where blossom
of late-flowered cherries
had stained grey pavement.

Further, a pine-coned path
snaked by grazed bark, the shins
of pines, and headlight shards
glinted over reddened earth.

These fragments of a car
or scooter come to grief
were more *memento mori*
of each bright thing's brief life.

That evening, walking home
across the castle site, I saw
grass stalks pierce crazed asphalt
like so many flashing swords,

a full moon scud through trees
above these green remains
of fortifications, its pale face
as in the local poet's lines.

2

A traffic-filled street in the city bears his name,
its glittering offices clearly seen
beyond this castle's fire-bombed gatehouse,
from an approach road cresting the rise
as it twists through outworks of a wooded mound.

Here was the place by which he'd mourned
changes under a vine-strewn wall,
the moon above the ruined castle
shining an unchanged, luminous glow
while for centuries that structure stood its ground.

So where is the brilliance of long ago?
No ghostly retainers or GI Joes
are transferred over white cars and coaches
convoying tourists by the switchback road
you climbed, fumes fog-like in these pines –
where the occupying armies once camped round.

3

Now when the emperor was restored
these trees were on the losing side:
their trunks, paralysed sentries;
leaves, plumes shaking in a breeze.

Holding the hill gave material advantage.
Power gravitated in an earlier age
to this natural fortress of river cliffs and gorges.
Partly dismantled by restoration forces,
the rest burnt down in a single bombing raid.
Inside its main defensive walls
a statue of the warlord on his horse
with one blind eye and helmet's crescent moon
overlooks the city's blinking neon.
Here his past reappears in simulation –
come back as a wheeling bird's eye view
of lookout towers, the banquet halls,
and peacock-painted sliding screens
are reconstructed as computer graphics
on a series of flickering video screens.

4

From a plinth in ornamental shrubbery
this dress–coated, bronze politician
has blank eyes fixed on an era of wars:
his selectively related histories
miss live experiments, rapes
when just remembered foreigners died
(however much it's denied, denied
by interested voices) and maps
could really point to places
where life was evil then, perhaps.

5

Bansui, you're their local poet not mine
with moon-viewing parties and blossom
of that late-flowered cherry, a pink stain
on grey pavement, glimpsed against the hum

coming through trees from a tour bus engine;
a uniformed girl at its door waves her pennant
beckoning veterans or children by the shrine
to their dead: it's what fleeting blossom meant;

and though some still insist it never was,
others have been ready to apologize at last
for the mounds of unearthed skulls, the burden

of documents in archives, stored or lost,
that would likely vindicate the poet Auden
in his journeying to and from those wars.

Japanese Watercolours

The glow of dawn behind a hill
rousing two thatched houses,
a lake boat's bed-sheet sail
set under snow-topped volcanoes,
tuned stones in meanders
of a stream as it wanders
past narrow canoes,
close reeds, the cranes
in flight above a bridge, black pines...

From bogeymen's humiliations
on rickety tenement stairs,
down snaking corridors I escaped
the dark disturbances –
and between my dozing parents lay
awake to roses on wallpaper,
or four thin slots' faint painted distance
diminishing those nightmares
in first hints of day.

Dream Report

Last night I dreamed of you, lost friend,
and in the dream you'd died;
the news had come as a relief
because at least I could mourn your loss,
so the grief made me feel good inside.

Upstairs, you showed a woodcut or print
which, despite not being an artist,
you'd worked on right to the end:
still the block wouldn't properly ink,
a child's head in outline not even penned.

With corkscrew hair falling into your eyes,
tired brow like a ploughed field under snow,
last night you returned in a dream, lost friend,
to relive brief confidences I've since missed
from a meeting that hadn't ever happened.

Days Before

Slowly, outside the locked door
of this premature baby clinic,
window frames and dusk make
sunlight squares move across a block floor.

Days before,
                    starting up from a nightmare
to find every stick of furniture stolen
and blinking to make it untrue, I'd seen
a similar, paler wood square
where the carpet should have been.

But that night my daughter was full of ideas;
there were so many things she wanted to tell me
and me, half asleep in the earliest dawn,
I was listening, I was all ears
as she told me, sat on my eiderdown,
that it's the children choose their own parents
– and she not even born.

In This Life

1

With the torque of a ceiling propeller
precarious as it drives still air
in this life, there's waking alone
on a far side of the globe or town;

there's waiting on benches, choked by routine,
to glimpse the new-born through a glass screen
and family matters we wanted to tell you
but had to postpone.

2

In this life there's no end of scars,
no end of being in the wars –
a car crash, brain surgery, now the caesarian
cut faintly marring your mother.

But in the other, we're walking near home
through outskirts flecked with shade and sun,
for though life itself's an idea
(naming, imagining you) it's one
the future will just have to play by ear.

On the Outskirts

This is the place of stubborn growth –

from a railway embankment's wall
through crevices of eaten-back cement
shrubs have pushed, horizontal
tufts on brickwork below a ruled sky;
alongside the gantries, a signal
sends express trains into the kitchens
of small, post-war family apartments;
here your mother spent her youth.

A factory gate's arch in curved concrete
carries the period, angular lettering;
day after day, all hell breaks loose
in the form of rumours from the hot street,
shouts, or screaming brakes which fit
not voices of accusers, we're used to that,
but the language in a tiny infant's cry.

It mingles with traffic on the bypass nearby
bringing to this city our far-fetched desires.
The steam shunter painted on a rusting sign
gives notice of a glass works' branch line
where, in the small hours, its engine
whistles to your tired waking parents.

Once, when a dance band rehearsed, we went
out to a full moon in still light sky;
it sharpened behind those power-lines' staves
as if serenading the new, earthly lives
with promise of fulfilments close at hand,
or at least recommending them to try.

Same World

Not like the family of caravans
parked for a night beside branch lines,
mechanical grabs gouging house foundations,
as you say, there's bound to be one
nostalgic for names of local firms on tins,
who tends greens by heaped pallets, machines
rusting among the reed heads' motions
on outskirts – small-scale industries
long since beaten to their knees.

As you say, there's bound to be one
who haunts flecked shadow while it lengthens,
finding relief in summer afternoons,
eager for the lift of a dance band's tunes
above distant lorries which enchants
this singular place, and just in time
as he has to leave; he's got to fly –
swallows above new developments
tumbling commas through a flushed sky.

For the infant asleep in her pram,
this one and the other who stays
examining weather at a window frame
are both as much part of the same
world with its grandpas, its dad and mum –
because there's the pace of allotments,
train timetables, wide-body planes,
rooted affections and longing to distance
commingled in her veins.

In the Consular Section

But the question was: what had made her cry,
faced with our documents spread on a table
and him there starting to read them?
Perhaps his large, coffee-stained teeth,
or irritated biro and matching accent?

Shelved encyclopedias? The almanacs?
A naval attaché of nineteen thirty-eight
who had, as it said on the marble plaque,
remained at his cruiser's battle station
dying heroically somewhere in the Med?

Her crying disturbed their off-white walls
hung with various sombre, framed views
(classical sites like the Temple of Concord)
so he could say, and without a smile,
our infant didn't want those banns read?

It brought the consul himself to sympathize.
Would their Japanese garden distract her?
Or the breast? There were winter trees,
a stone urn, ducks on an ornamental lake.
It seemed the best for one of us to take her.

Then, in quiet streets of an embassy district
she was almost herself again at once –
hard to believe the red carpet and effect
of diplomatic mail-bags or echoey walls
and a voice hadn't made her take offence.

Out of Circulation

So I telephone ahead to rent a car,
queasy, having never learnt to drive;
but without any need of it, I arrive
at a guesthouse in the north country,
the place somehow familiar
with its steeply sloping street,
slate tiles and sash windows
all glimpsed from a dormer in the roof –
choppy angles like a petrified sea.

By a dining table's thick white cloth,
the regulars set me at my ease.
I *am* at ease, suddenly home now
after years out of circulation;
but the friend I've come to meet,
a composite of various people
we don't hear from, months on end,
is half lost in the crowd somehow,
hesitant, not making himself known.

I stoop down to pick up a coin
or commemorative medal. It's foreign:
every *U* of the lettering has *V*.
Then I offer the thing in an open palm.
Their faces grow vacant before me.
It's not that I meant to provoke
but they think I'm having them on,
and this bronze emblem, heavy Italian,
if it's not theirs, it must be mine…

which is when I woke.

TWO

Boundary Drive

for Matt Simpson

1

If distance makes our city
a landscape of the mind,
mine could almost be
the view at your window
that blustery March day.
It was just the place I'd known
from other points of vantage:
a bleary traipse at dawn
or London train's passage;
come home to, any way,
they're triangulated now
with a rough field or two,
house backs, ruffled trees
and diminishing hedgerow,
roof-lines, the factories
fringed by remnants of farm;
estuary landscape, its high
percentages of sky
and beckoning horizon make me
inescapably who I am
still, though still I try.

2

Things we have in common
kept coming up like Bootle
childhoods, foreign wives,
the Backs, the Studio School…
Here, for a firm long gone,
I worked nights as a watchman,
walked Speke Boulevard
while the airport tower
turned art deco cardboard
cut-out under clouds that lour,
profusely bleed or blush –

as if those shapes in passing
pale avenues and drives
comment on the scene below.
Scattered pedestrians lean
in fresh gusts that blow
more cloud across the pane,
bring storm-light to an afternoon
of alternate sun and rain
where seagulls' white glints flash
(it ended with the rainbow
your wife had foreseen).

3

But the scurrying forms
patterned by shade and sun
are twisted with qualms,
equally commented on
by city fringe's concrete
blocks, brick crescents, asphalt
fates the planners write;
their optimistic-to-a-fault
meanings meant to stay
are street names on a map
of Bootles change would swallow.
Outside, by a loading bay
boys huddle now the wind
abolishes last thoughts of play
in their interrupted game:
high time to push off home.
As fading light impinged
at curtains, what took shape,
in the course of views exchanged
between one who'd to go
and another staying behind,
moved on from its frame.

Aftershocks

1

That year college started late;
pigeons fed on uncut lawn
about a reminiscent court,
its peonies in full bloom.

Mock frontages, a cross
between Italian seminary
and New England campus,
sported scaffolding, débris –
silence by each damaged classroom.

2

There were crazes in façades
of burnt ochre, sienna rooftiles
hung with wisteria flowers
like parma violet waterfalls
and the small, untended shrine
had staggered like a salaryman,
pine pillars lifted off their stone
bases, all its saké downed.

3

From music school windows
came phrases, tricky scales
on disparate pianos
practising western intervals.

A cornet joined them as I waited,
discords struck with every note
promising unstated
concertos, but that bit more remote.

4

Last night it rained so heavily
the sound was of high winds
clattering leaves.
                    Not dogs or cats,
they say it's raining husbands
– as if for these girl graduates
trooping under massed umbrellas
like in Hiroshige, like in Utamaro,
past the stooping gardeners
who, wet leaves hard to brush away,
will doggedly take up birch brooms
and sweep at them tomorrow.

5

In the garden of the Bard
we found wormwood, wormwood,
a medlar, apricock and may tree.
But where was rue? Where rosemary,
rosemary, that's for remembrance?

6

Whether it was oreoles
that descant from thick foliage,
or some local souls
at work once more in old age
who whistled on their knees,
I heard survival's celebration
tormenting those with a relation
or two, with whole families
in just twenty seconds gone.

7

We were counting their losses,
their good luck or lack of it
in a wall on the top of a car,
toppled houses and intact ones
side by side in city blocks
like random bombed sites
with phone numbers and names
on signs at the edge of cleared plots
among odd stones and mosses,
minute gardens' flowerpots.

8

The noise of clearing up
came like so many aftershocks;
streets were jammed with dumper trucks,
skips; we kept on hearing
splintered rending cracks
of written-off wood houses
as dainty grabs and bulldozers
moved in on caterpillar tracks.

9

Shaken to its foundations,
the idea of identity's
in mourning for some grounds.
On fields of ashes it dissolves
back fifty years' enduring, a nation's
concrete fissured in these sounds:
'We stopped believing the authorities,
stopped believing in ourselves.'

10

'Real swallows,' you exclaimed
as they nimbly dipped and climbed
over river banks, cemented in;
Mount Rokko erased by mist
like apartments swathed with polythene
commanded this crushed area;
another late-flowering cherry
shed its petals under drizzle,
but I missed the araucaria
(that primitive monkey-puzzle tree).

11

Yellow powder on your nose
was the pollen of camellias:
so perhaps the Muses
are still memory's girls
– as suddenly appears
with a couple of cabbage
whites like flying blossom,
an address book's double page
spread, my last five years'
lives filling them.

12

Beyond the lamp-lit circle
and after-dinner talk,
red blazes of azaleas
were breathing in the dark.

As if the lost returned
to make a last goodbye…
They reach us through fresh bushes
shaping up outside.

Italian in Sendai

Not long after the rainy season's start
our breakfast-time weather report
predicted a deficiency of sunlight
– as if you needed to be told,
with that patter interrupting grey quiet
and every umbrella unfurled.

Lilting gestures, cadenced words
said what you thought of glass façades,
of buildings clad in toilet-tile,
cheek by jowl with a tin or wood shack
when all your life it's been campanile,
stucco, responsive plasterwork.

Curtains had opened on another cool spell;
you and I, like mercenary soldiers
accumulating reasons to go home,
were defenceless against nostalgias
piled with the clouds on some
closed horizon, knowing only too well

that a bottle of wine's not Italy
nor foreigner speaking your language, home,
and the sound made by coffee
bubbling in a machine's upper part
is no better than a short, translated poem –
even if I've learnt it off by heart.

The Explanation

White marble gleams through privet hedges
on both sides of the carriageway.
Wrappers, newsprint, litter stay
unshifted by wind on mown grass verges

in blobs of shadow from copper beech trees'
clotted-blood-colour leaves, the sky
half blotted out in a late July
that brings back, uncalled for, the scraped knees

of childhood. They were bleeding and gritty
as I pulled a bike with twisted frame,
its front wheel buckled, down these same
avenues through outskirts of this city.

Just now, in a gap across from the Crem
giving onto a garden or farmyard,
a peacock and a rabbit stared
out of their home ground. I glanced at them

in passing. They remain like neat scars
because I'd been going at a pace
to notice and remember. So the place
made itself known, pretended to be ours,

and we at least could perhaps understand
that gravestones, foliage, accidents give
life to these forms which live, if they live,
on a rabbit, a peacock, on whatever comes to hand.

Scargill House

1

On a route North, one Friday night
we took the right side of the river;
familiar climbing turns with tight
corners of barns had led us straight
past the gate and curving drive
of Scargill House, its off-white
pebble dash, blue slate roof
the same as when I'd come alive
on springy limestone turf.

2

Brought by bus with the parish young wives
or Mother's Union, we'd first glimpse,
brave above pines across the Wharfe valley,
its chapel's inverted V
and, rising behind, the craggy hills
from whence I really thought our help
cometh on summer holidays,
when even shaky perspectives
of Sunday painters' easels
were heartfelt hymns of praise.

3

It all depended on the weather,
for though the dry stone walls
of sodden sheep tracks echoed
with our folk song rhymes,
the family's spirit failed;
there'd be no knowing whether
it was us or Malham Tarn,
like Leah, had been veiled
in a cloud of rain and mist.

4

If you have the talent, use it –
that was a lesson I tried to learn
as from Dick Marsh, the warden.

He'd led us in prayer and been our host
down pot holes, on hill walks – was lost
in a freak rock climbing accident…
like the man who founded his house on a cliff,
because whoever would find life
must, of course, first lose it.

5

Swimming in the Wharfe
one summer with the faithful
– but what was that palaver
where the bridge's grey stone curved?

It was just my doused, saved,
gasping father
landed on the river bank, a small
and shaken mortal.

6

Who gave me the *Apocrypha*?
Faith turned into scholarship's
romance of the obscure.
                        I'd suffer
'My Cherie Amour' on Rachel's lips
just to be dreaming of the other
things we'd done or left undone,
their punishments in *Revelation*
by St John, the Apocalypse.

7

Waking, twenty-six years later,
I suddenly remembered one
idyllic afternoon
we wandered through Grass Woods,
then paddled in the stream
– all ruined when she lost her watch,
though whether in the dense grass cover
or smooth-flowing river
(and we searched both bank and water)
that present from her Gran had gone;
the moment and the time had gone for ever.

8

Car headlight beams from a minor road,
snaking back the length of the dale's
far side, would search through trees,
for an instant reveal
two teenagers apart, as if
caught in a freeze-frame photograph
on the copse's edge.
                        In memory's
re-run version, I know that the one
who's lifted a blue rugby jersey
and bared her breasts at the August moon
is my first wife to be.

9

For what might have been a last chance,
I stumbled up to Kettlewell
along the river as night fell.
When we met, she was keeping her distance.

It had seemed a vain attempt to recover
someone I wasn't about to lose
in twenty-one years, who chose
to persevere with her stumbling lover.

10

Those years later, we had gone
by a patch of mown green
edged with grey, cut stone
where a chapel once had been,
down an arbour of limes
flanked by graveyard statues,
defunct tombs, like our times
and about as much use
– except that memory stirs
lumps of unburied past
and what we had made waste,
with that punning voice of hers.

11

Familiar turns had led us straight
past the gate and curving drive
of Scargill House, its blue
slate roof, white pebble dash
through autumn's gathered gloom.

From the dark of our friend's car,
in attempts at one last glimpse
of its circular conference room,
I twisted round, so couldn't see
if she had glanced back too.

12

But that night, further North
as we fronted blazing skies
above the Yorkshire Moors,
neither one of us foresaw
that we would reach an end
so flaming and definitive
there'd be no making amends,
no shared past to restore.

The Late

i.m. Donald Davie

Nobody's under the hill tonight
silhouetted up ahead.
The beams of each car headlight
(blurred in a rush hour's fetid air)
pick out pines along the climb;
they shine, then disappear.

I'm tired after work and winded
by the sudden death of someone
I hoped to impress or improve on,
who helped me, and I had let down.
'So what did you expect?' he said,
'– Flowers all the way?'

Nobody's under the hill tonight,
except that each car headlight ray
picks me out then squirms away
and in the deeper dark, he's gone.
Nobody's under the hill tonight:
you're really on your own.

Winter Interiors

for John and Christine Roe

1

Waking to low-angled sunlight
aglow in white curtains, in a sliding screen,
on wooden-framed and sand-encrusted wall,
to the smell of a loaf baked overnight
and, despite the season, kept from harm
in that devastated city of all places,
I lift my good ear from the pillow, turn
(as if no longer needing to yearn
for anything more) and find the warm,
steady-breathing faces
of a mother and child in your chilly room.

2

Though just now, unseasonable snows
like frozen spume on a Hokusai wave
have whitened out the distances,
draped pine branches with their ermine –
though we are not all states, all princes,
and there's never been another School of Love –
back to the days of numbed senses
at condensation-beaded windows,
we're giving it our best to survive;
though never very good at close family,
at accepting dependence because strong enough,
in the still of a difficult winter, who knows?
Perhaps we're learning to be.

For My Daughter

'We all of us love Miss Matty, and I somehow
think we are all of us better when she is near us.'
Elizabeth Gaskell

This morning at the breakfast table,
what was it about a crow
perched on satellite antennae
above an ice cream tub of snow
caught my daughter's eye?

Below the blackness of that bird,
once more appears our yellow
water tank smeared with rust;
upon a white scoop-full's overflow
the same crow comes to rest.

She points, laughs infectiously,
then clutches at her temples;
it seems for my daughter our world's
a mass of picture-book examples,
and we supply the words.

★

This morning at the breakfast table,
they frame a snowy landscape for us:
its quintessence of nothing, a sparrow's
mishap in suburbs, the various
ways of looking at blackbirds or crows…

Does a bundle of accident and incoherence
alter our morning's breakfast scene?
or the spirit her laughter brings?
You may well laugh, but laugh again
at these ordinary arrangements of things.

Dandelion Clocks

Stooping to my daughter's height,
I get a glimpse of how it looks
this close to ants, or a cabbage white;
I'm blowing dandelion clocks
(as you might pluck petals off a daisy)
and with every breathed-out puff,
murmur 'She loves me not…she loves me…'
while the separate blobs of fluff
drift among each grass stalk's seed-head,
take their chances with the other
wildings sent on currents of town air,
just as her own great-grandfather
had grown up hurt in his sisters' care,
silently resentful and embittered –

yet from him sprang what family we are.

THREE

Via Sauro Variations

for O.

'…notre destin qui t'étonne
Se joint au jour qui va finir'
Guillaume Apollinaire

1

Despairingly, you asked would I like to live *there*
as we drove in or out through swollen suburbs:
hypermarket parking, tower-blocks, shrubbery,
geometric shapes and reflections in the air.

Surfaces of ochre, brick red, a plaster grey
had been taken from an architect's prize sketches
– enough to suppose this Emilian city's edges
were a few lines on some paper by Paul Klee.

2

Well no; how could you love
that place after all those years
just minutes from the main square's
cafés, four flights up above
this long and narrow street
with its open shop doorways?

Curious proprietors gaze
at passers-by who meet
a schoolfriend or acquaintance,
step close against the wall
expressing surprise – as if all
life itself weren't an off-chance
encounter, a second glance.

3

Outside, youth's vagrant chatter
washes along the street below;
to close a slatted shutter
you climb from interior shadow
in pyjamas, on to a chair,
stand out against another clear night
over roof-tiles; in the lit square
of that window your thin silhouette
for a moment plainly reaches.

4

Recalling my appearance in that darkness –
who, hesitating, came back to the floor,
I'm what was reflected on silvered glass
of a wardrobe mirror by your door.

In the face will have been fear –
of what might follow, immediate or late,
but also desire, abandoned, still great,
to approach and reach near

an original, translate distances
in the miscarried language we say,
and even know ourselves in all senses –
as I hurried down the passageway.

5

Yet still those ten days shared
were put by like a hidden gift
as if this life would not forget us,
although there seemed nothing left
to give but a few brief letters
in a syntax that made little sense
and two signed books, the souvenirs
of a brief affair: no recompense
for the unlived or the ill-lived years.

6

You drove us in that aftermath
to Bagno-Vignoni, its small town
square a therapeutic thermal bath
in which we were to drown
all remaining nostalgia beneath
Tarkovsky's greens and brown.

The Maremman town, it was no dream;
by wooden-raftered loggia, liquid sound,
I watched the bubbling waters steam,
peered at a camera, the bitter end
of our story, our musical theme –
we seemed about to comprehend.

7

Under Populónia, the site custodian
approached us with today's dog barking
and excavated mounds, Etruscan tombs
outfacing a somnolent horizon.

'So have you noticed any ghosts?'
teasing me, you said; our pasts,
and not the sum of faults, returned
(if faults do die when they're confessed)
to a sculpted ancient married couple,
the look of fierce repose between them,
couched together on their funeral urn.

8

Walking back near upturned hulls,
wicker pots, cork floats, all this gear:
the dusty clutter of another era,
I came to where you lay asleep
on pebbles by the curving shore.

Intending a heap of fish-scraps
on the finished restaurant plate –
'My bed's a boneyard,' I had said
and, understanding, blushed: perhaps
you hadn't heard; whereas we of course…

Here were different pasts to give me pause.

9

Looking for a place to eat
in August, closed-for-the-holiday season,
we were directed to a narrow street
beyond deep shadows of a portico.

The restaurant ceiling had Zodiac signs –
blind struggle in the network of stars,
like the dry leaf on a rain-blotched car's
sun-roof, yes, and one more sign –

there by the wooden street door
on a bell push still, that name I love,
not to be rung but conjuring the memory
I still have desires, enough to need no more.

10

A thick mist on the Padana plain
did away with distances
that morning I took an early train;
it seemed the chances
of following outlines of trees
past farms and onion campanili
had been stolen from me
by the weather; still, possibilities
hidden in years' silences
might have waited to emerge
with filter plants at a field ditch edge,
though patches of the dewy grass
is all there was to see.

11

Arriving early at that door
gave me a chance to shake his hand
(just leaving from one more weekend).
Inside, despite refurbishing,

kitchen and rooms were as of old
with pink-flecked grey stone tiles,
postcard boxes, work-space, box-files,
a bedside lamp to distinguish me, wishing.

You kept blinds and windows open
to let fresh spring air circulate.
It held a hope of not being too late,
though doubtless the future would scold me –

coming and disturbing how things were before.

12

Like a convalescent from that well-known malady
I strolled around Salsomaggiore,
loitering *carabinieri* before me
and thoughts, a rare old gentleman or lady
out for their constitutional breaths
of fresh air by babylonian baths,
elegant bars, grey louvred shutters…
I was wondering what it might be most matters
and overtook a squabbling pair
with coiffured poodle in the town's main square.

13

We crossed a bridge above the Taro's bed.
Weathered statues on each parapet
were glimpsed and lost as the road's unfolding let
grievances, then quieter things be said

of chances in lives too long postponed.
Unravelling examples, what we heard
(whimpers and yapping) was a pet's hospital:
all around, sick animals groaned.

You had pointed out land-slip and rockfall
while stepping across fresh furrows;
but an earth-mover's rusty yellows
came lurching behind to have the last word.

14

Then came the simple problem
of switches, someone's name
gasped forgetting who I am,
shadow on a wall, a windscreen
wiper to put out of mind,
each unfamiliar obstacle
to overcome if we're to find
the other in each other's soul.

Yes, words are tender things.
To reach out of the solitudes
was hard, being ourselves,
but harder still to cry
from happiness, or laugh
convulsively at a relief
in being found again and try
again and try and try.

15

Escaping from the sleepless heat
of Via Sauro, late July,
I saw the tendons of bare knees
respond as you changed gear
and, glancing from the passenger seat
at one of those two candidates
for the Charterhouse of Parma,
guessed this had to be the route
taken those eight years before
back to Verona, distances

blurring in a sudden downpour,
windscreen wipers unable to cope
as, recalling insufficient fear,
I fled what seemed impossible;
we'd said goodbye, assuming a calm
like lovers driven away from their senses –
as I was again, into the storm.

16

Part-way across a reservoir lake
I'm tired; waves are stronger
suddenly, distances longer,
and empty since an earthquake
that house stands on the hill –
another predictable mistake,
its dilapidated empty shell
like this future's startled look.

As the chilly current hampers
my progress with its flow –
no turning back, there's more
that way where Romans go
home towards tents or campers –
how you turn and reassure…

17

Strings of bulbs between each frontage,
white, with a fainter halo in the air,
meant more than Christmas angels
or the colourful tail of a falling star.

It was almost like driving with fog-lamps,
oncoming dangers made manifest
through greyness enshrouding roadsigns,
vehicles, branches in a lake of mist.

Frost glazed Via Sauro; late morning
fed illusions of lives without want;
as if the weather had a sense of humour,
like a disease, fog came and went.

18

Wind cutting at a stranger's ankles
down this dark and cobbled street,
the start of someone coughing
echoes after sounds of feet.

I thought it would hold us together
renewing a married embrace?
But no, come between us,
the cold exacts its price.

19

You called me out at the sound of a band
and there they were: drum-majorettes,
musicians themselves and, a little behind,
a tractor was towing a white wedding cake
on a float with the carnival queen,
small children disguised as family pets
and a clown wore a black stain on his cheek
as if where a tear had been.

We had come through a difficult winter
with news of survivors in a shelled city;
dubious hopes and speechless forebodings
rose in the air at the thrown confetti.
This annual rite would invite us to enter
into the spirit of things.

20

For somebody come through a difficult winter
waiting for his tricky operation,
perhaps because a kindness is done
to homeless from the nearby civil war,
or an old man drops his money in the square,
sees it fluttering about him on a breeze,
passersby help him pick it up but what's more
when he gets to the bank and counts it, it's all there,
Parma, can't your contradictions please?

21

The lake in the Parco Ducale
had been drained of mysteries:
thin branches of felled trees
withered on raked gravel, ducks,
carp and swans quite spirited away.

And all in aid of some renewal,
we'd stopped at its crumbled margin,
gazed down where the fat-fed fish
were pursuing their own ends,
at ringlets of disturbance, tried
to touch those depths still without harm.
What were they but a murky calm
choked by algae, infestations?

22

On the island, soil erosion
showed how trunks and branches
were fed by thin, splayed fingers
reaching under a dry earth crust
where tufts of grass, small huts and mosses
formed a backdrop for the avenue.

Placed among cascading leaves
were figures, scrolls, shell basins
of a fountain in full view,
these marble sculptures badly smeared
as if with thick mascara –
but their tears had all been dried.

23

Ten years back, we took this line.
The train from Parma to Monterosso
just couldn't get there soon enough
for me, and maybe you, those years ago.

Arrived, we did what the infatuated do,
booked a hotel and, being alone then,
fell, as I hoped we would, in love.
This far into that different future,
one September day, we came on purpose
but stumbled upon the place again by chance.
Ten years back, it had taken all the force
of feeling and circumstance.

24

Crammed walls were resilient enough
to survive those few years' silence;
we'd squeeze past furniture or glance
around at each framed photograph:

the landscapes, sunsets, ancestors...
signs of an independent life
crying out loud not to be left
alone; here, on the chest of drawers

a mirror speckled at its edges
contains me a moment, the ghost
of years ago who loved and lost
and gained dependents by slow stages.

25

It was not the place I loved –
no tinkling chimes, ivy buds,
coral clasps or amber studs,
the landlady's property shoved
into an alcove, every room
bare of variegated leaves
where a spider's web survives
you'd unhook with a broom,
taking possession, as if to prove
by a corridor full of shadows
one last time now shutters close,
it's not the place I love.

FOUR

Something to Declare

for James Lasdun

Last off the flight out of Amsterdam,
I was asked, all casual like,
where it was we'd come from...
But the customs officer's sniffer dog
needed no time on some holiday wear.
Passports controlled, we took the Blue Channel
with not a thing, as usual,
(apart from the tiredness, incipient jet lag)
nothing to declare –

except that on these skylines
as in a recurrent dream
ghosts of Burtonwood aerodrome,
a closed asylum's crenellations,
flashes, grassed heaps, road signs
made themselves felt with local tones
painlessly understood.

But mostly it was agitated leaves
flapping at reflections on a window pane,
or late June light that lingers
over heaped cumulus after rain;
like a conversation, rudely interrupted,
they come through with an answer
drawing out what it is to be
in this home again.

Your Other Country

Love, this is your other country
in the middle of its summer:
a rusted siding or a spur
is choked with rampant willowherb;
round a front door, sparrows disturb
body armour of large ivy leaves
as they flutter from under cottage eaves
at dusk; hereabouts, B and Bs
have windows with 'No Vacancies',
and evening shadows stretch us on
speckled brick, or paving stone.

Along the walls, the old defences,
practically stepping in my own footsteps,
we were grazed by light that says
more about us than corner shops
grown gentrified or bricked-up now;
here, feet still descend worn stairs
leading where pleasure boats glide
and a thing you'd never seen,
horses move on a fairground ride
unmoved by the started jigsaw scene
I put aside to try another.

You see I'm a tourist here myself,
a tourist in your other country,
but glancing into gardens, see
from trimmed lawns, local genii
of place and language rise to say
words about how the sharp-tongued
must fear those with good memories,
how even the colouring of the past
comes back and is prolonged
by witty remarks from the Seventies;
then, tactfully, they slip away.

Since You Asked

Just an excursion down to Poole Harbour;
but searching back over the way we came
for a turquoise necklace didn't disturb our
afternoon on Brownsea in the bay.

When a peacock patrolling the seaside
woke me from my sunstruck daydream
of yachts towards Old Harry's Rocks,
it was just a few feet from the tide.

What would Hardy have made of today,
of the peacock stalking along that shore
when a lost turquoise necklace meant more
than perhaps even he could say?

The Bargain

Once, in a junk shop along the Albert Road,
amongst old soldiers' medals, uniforms,
the perished gas masks, heaped-up furniture
from clearances, and defunct family hoards
of pottery, paperbacks, some stuffed birds,
or records no one wanted any more –
I stumbled on a few job lots of words.

Naturally enough, they'd seen better days
and smelt quite high, but you never can tell
when a word will come in handy…Well,
although the chap there said he'd no idea
where the stuff came from (filling in for someone),
as he told me I could have them for a song
I knocked him down a bit and took them home.

Curious to see what I'd bought, needless to say,
I tipped my plastic bag out on the table
and there, *disarmed, inert, inarticulate,* they lay:
province, bungalow, pale, slogan, char, veranda,
abacus, divan, dosh, audit, serf, indenture,
annihilate, cancel, snuff, silence, disappear,
not to mention ones like *station, race* or *gender.*

Why not clean them up, they'll be as good as new?
Then I borrowed Brasso, silver polish, perfume;
yet no amount of elbow grease or corporation pop
would cut through centuries of use and blame.
So I took them back along the Albert Road,
but the man had gone, the owner didn't want them,
and no one else either, though I tried every shop –

'Sorry, mate,' they said, 'we've already got the same.'

Playing Dead

'He paints words with the past'
                                Roy Fisher

They're exhaust-caked privet colours,
lupin heads and brick dust
tracked through the glazes that time
formicas on a feel for things
like cough drops, bubble gum,
black liquorice, things with the taste
of four farthings about them,
things which aren't likely to last –
but then do, the pink or the grey
I'd just go on chewing, though
losing so quickly its flavours
through a bright, cold winter day –
mum's plum jam on an aspirin
or dandelion and burdock, bringing
back, red-flecked, the yellow
and blue of an old black eye:
'Well now, who's this in the wars?'

There were corrugated iron roofs,
daubed fences frayed with rust,
a purple forehead, badly bruised
walking right into a lamp post.
I lay pretending to be dead
under the vapour trails' white
in an ominous or mackerel sky –
but no Red Indian found me,
so I got up and walked away.
Years passed, became the compost
of time's intentness rotted down
with whatever it was I used
to slip between pedestrian fears
of policemen and dark alleys,
railway lines, the waste ground,
talking to strangers, school bullies –
whatever I use to get back home.

Die Lilliputbahn

for Diethard Leopold

It wasn't roasted chestnuts in their cones,
a roller-coaster's ups and downs
or that famous ferris wheel's slow turns,
but the quiet of the Lilliputbahn's
station platform, where we sat
until the train arrived, which came
to represent for me Vienna's quiet.

Because they had taken a piece of its heart
during the seven German years,
if through the Prater's woods a train's
going in mist with an echo of voices,
its clatter among the leaves explains
why quiet on that station platform
came to represent Vienna's quiet.

I'm taking exactly what can't be undone
to hurl it, at least in a manner of speaking,
into a future, as trees on the turn
will bear this summer's memories
but hint while they do of a chill to come.
We had arrived by the Lilliputbahn.
I was listening in to Vienna's quiet
among the leaves of an early autumn.

Zoo Time

It doesn't occur that often –
we're brought from the daily routine
of being mucked out and fed, unseen
for years on end, backdated now
by theme park jungle and stately home;
but sometimes we're suddenly on show,
caught, as the gleam from a window
for a moment catches Harry Lime;
true, there's something of shame or crime
about our exposure, though mostly it's more
a Caspar Hauser from his cell,
or petrified rabbit in a headlamp beam.
Another voice is speaking us:
we're a Disney natural history short,
Johnny Morris on 'fifties TV,
domestic–sentimental, the lightly humorous.
In fact, we sound a bit like you and me.

It seems they're not supposed to feed us,
but sometimes we're offered a crust
or curiously asked, 'Are you depressed?'
I could envy the famous animals
for whom it seems more *Show Time*,
the albatross and woodworm, stars
like Rilke's panther on display
who constantly paces round his cage,
till no world starts beyond the bars
making him appear centre stage.
For most of us there's nothing for it,
nothing but to turn away,
drift off with barely a backward glance
to where in our natural habitat, a state
of isolation, anonymity, of distance,
we're sometimes still given the chance,
somehow, to communicate.

Back to Work

for Hiroshi Ozawa

Nothing, for years, but a concrete slab
straddled the river's reinforced banks;
cars would slow to meet the ranks
of on-coming traffic at a bridge
with narrow walkway by its edge,
supports of rust-smeared cement,
red piers sun-faded and drab.

Beside it, now, a new bridge veers.
Houses were razed from out its path,
flat land resculpted to embed
a blue span that one slab supports.
There, the streams of vehicles go
uninterrupted, while, overhead,
hawks dip towards a rippling flow
of water round boulders beneath.

At the foot of its steep approach mound,
a lamp post, bits of abandoned curb
and pitted asphalt emerge from ground;
they mark which way the old street went.
One summer's been more than enough
for weeds to cover this sloping patch
of scrubland above the river bend
beyond fencing by a baseball pitch;
and here, among tufts of grass,
all but hidden, a short-cut starts.

You can pick it out if you know
from the few blades trodden down,
raw soil, or an odd scraped stone;
then it joins that remnant of road.
Persistent there, a wind-sown shrub
has forced itself through cracks
between the choked gutter and kerb.

Each day I take these neglected ways,
convenient beyond tennis courts,
walk under the slope bulldozers raised
and let my thoughts
move with gusted leaves, the curve
of river that cut this open space
bound by tree-lined heights, a cliff face
with its TV mast towering above.

For a moment between obligations
and feeding where it can, my time
is mine to alight on what you will:
ancestral tombs in a pine-tree shroud,
castle remains on the opposite hill;
but then once, at that rising parapet,
a colleague appeared as if from the world –
'Have you finished your work?' he called,
and me, awakened from my daydream,
'No, I'm just going back to it.'

Only a moment between obligations
unremembered for months, I admit;
yet it's on just such a piece of land
scattered with weeds, leaves lying around,
between the new bridge approach's mound
and dirt patch of a baseball ground,
that, passing, I would make my stand.

Still Life Portraits

Late November morning sun
comes low above the hills,
through pine branches, spills
across a block floor's wooden
squares, and elongated
shadows from the furniture
make slatted patterns, pure
tone, a thing unsaid.

Table legs, the backs of chairs
and window frames have lent
forms for guitar strings, a fret-board,
chess moves; the spider plant
leaves are a world map's air routes
to spots we had or hadn't been
on the double-page spread
of a flight magazine.

But not off anywhere, for once,
with playing child and mother,
like a fern's fresh, coiled shoots
you allow yourself this truce
in the season's worsening weather:
our shadows all over the floor
for some minutes, an hour, more,
are displayed across these other
facets of existence.

FIVE

Marking Time

1

In marking time, the errors come
so thick and fast we're at a loss
to count or, laughing, to recount them;
some I recognize, because
they're mine, mine word for word.
With only this to do, it's hard
marking time till the baby's born,
exams are over and I can return
to a family grown without me around.
I'm marking time to clear debts.
Across waste spaces comes the sound
of a high school marching band.
Freezing cold drum majorettes
stamp the dirt of a football pitch.

2

Beyond fogged windows in an overheated room
winter's losing its grip: for days
the treacherous turned to wetness,
then froze, ice crazing a pane;
it retreated by inches, and what was
dead in us through these last years –
frost patches where the sun doesn't reach,
ploughed piles of exhausted black snow –
wouldn't die, but remained, and is still.
You watch your step down under the hill;
to encourage the others, make examples of words,
as in high-walled back gardens loud birds
mean changes, marking time, and here we go.

Coat Hanger

Pegging out shirts on my first-floor balcony,
I happen to notice a white, wire coat hanger
dangling from one low branch of the tree
right by our neighbour's garden.
What's it doing there?

★

Perhaps it's a homage to Jasper Johns
for six months here in the Korean War,
or in memory of the feelings of his friend
who remembered a 'loneliness' from seven years before
'drifting into my ears off Sendai in the snow…'
(but where he saw that whiteness during August '45
I don't for the life of me know).

★

Well, yes, I suppose it could be mine,
blown about by a wind
that unhooks the things you can hang on a line
or bough: an abandoned black plastic umbrella,
the strips of white paper containing bad fortunes,
tied in neat bows, transferred to the tree
– which seems to have absorbed them;
spirited away the luck; at any rate, survived.

★

Though camouflaged, now
that one more layer of overlapping greens
has painted out winter, some distant love's
skin can still be glimpsed through freckled tones
of bark, sap, chlorophyll; like a phantom limb,
tanned patches come, pale down, a hand –
and so much else that could depend
on a coat hanger among the leaves.

Heavy Weather

'**Alone**, *adj.* In bad company.'
Ambrose Bierce

Not under a cloud, but in one,
I'm making heavy weather
of the rainy season, its
trampolines with droplets
strung between shrubs' leaves;
where steam climbs up through forest,
spiders' webs, fog particles
form in great floods from the past
like branches reaching through thick mist;
there comes no end of a problem
as traffic murmurs below a grey sky
now it's the rainy season,
which is to be endured, though
I'm making heavy weather of it.

Already, a year has gone.
Distressed to be told that alone
I've so little by way of resources,
you cannot see the compliment
in being wanted quite that much;
and I'm forced to admit
dependence isn't pretty.

Again in the heat, humidity,
stillness this June without breath
of wind, from a depth of summer,
here you are, you listen,
here respond, now, let it run
on, confront the mustiness,
black spots in a wall, foxed pages
and the white fur over leather –
as around us, heavy weather
turns just bearable at last.

An Interior Life

1

Just imagine, for a moment,
this curtain flapping at a window;
it interrupts oblique sun rays
from a summer dusk, the sky
washed clean by sudden rain,
and floating about the room's high corner
comes shadow like wrinkles under an eye
– as if a sense of depth were made
not by the damage time sketches,
but simply alternating light and shade.

2

Just so, and for a moment,
a moment not to be repeated,
the light of that 8:30 sunset
slants across the people seated
at a dinner table – faces,
their kept secret histories
not of what was cultivated
(eyes closed, dozing over pages)
no, but all you're fated
to be left with when you lose
the cheeks enlivened by this glow,
a wine, and swallowed phrases
in mouths shaped on the local accent...

3

It falls across two photographs,
each in a varnished frame:
the granddad dead some thirty years
(who dies again the instant
anyone recalls him alive)
and his late widow, the same,
whose cupboards still release such scent
as brings her back a while.

At La Villetta

i.m. Norma Buldini
Maria Teresa Sereni

Through acres of plain or veined marble
in overwrought styles, we came face to face
with that strong-willed distant look of the survivor
staring at a camera in her ninetieth year.

The light still gleamed by its oval frame.
Her daughter removed limp flowers from an urn,
arranged ones sold outside just to bring her.
She dusted the stone with unusual care.

A great granddaughter restless in her pushchair,
the mother unable to stifle a tear...
How long was it decent to linger?
What on earth were we all doing here?

★

The other was far less easy to find.
Though at the funeral, he couldn't remember.
In the end, we went back to the cemetery office.
They gave us the gist: a tomb number.

She asked for no photo, no pious quotation,
no tiny electric 'eternal flame' –
only the slab, two dates, her name.
No one had left any flowers behind.

No rustle of leaves, no bird calls, no sound
came from the stone-, smoke-, the ash-coloured sky.
No wan smile, no hand would likely appear
from the wall of the dead and astonish or snatch us.

There was nothing to keep you here.

Some Notes

After lunch, when the city slept,
I followed them into an empty square
– my wife and our two daughters,
one stumbling, one in her pushchair.
Near the music school, a pianist
was practising cadenzas.
                          On the air
chord cascades came, just us listening
to storms of notes, Rachmaninov,
that flurried on each neglected thing.
The cube of sky was clear enough,
a summer day's promises kept;
pigeons had paused on the fountain rim,
leaf shadow mottling its stone.
                          A bar's
street door was still open, the music
pouring around that close darkness
of polished chrome and glass
where somebody silently watches.
It recalls what the years have been like,
what's to come, or briefly it charms
the here, the now.
                          I read old love names
scored in a bench's wood, and time's
signatures marked by white splotches,
stains; the pianist repeats her phrases,
alters attack till satisfied with how
it went, or goes, or should go –
how it went or it goes or should go.

Qui

for Wallis Menozzi

Even the litter-bins know where they are:
all stencilled with the one word *qui*,
as if telling citizens 'here you are'
(here across a children's playground,
here at the corner of an empty street)
or, better, inviting them and us to treat
these places like we would our home.

Through an August's dead weight, cranes
are balanced in the stillness and heat
above each excavated building site,
brick infill or shell of concrete;
the days themselves too difficult to lift,
we scurry like ants among salt grains:
no sooner arrived than about to leave.

Yet, sometimes, perhaps late afternoon,
passing a bomb-site in the heart of town
that's waited fifty years to have
its barely started project halted,
or hurrying along by the stadium
after more talk in a quiet room
when stubborn local irritations
(every spot nursing its peculiar ones)
have unsuspectedly been melted,
again I notice them, never that far.

Here, even the litter bins know where they are.

Parco Nord

'In a half-finished park –
look, the boys attack saplings
with their sticks and stones.'

1

This half-finished park in the suburbs
is paved with good intentions:
benches, waste bins have been set
underneath wall-less pavilions;
rocks like bits of meteorite
are ranged down paths near rows
of splinted trees, their branches
linked by a swagging black hose.

2

No, the park's not prepossessing.
You can see its low brick walls
already sporting sprayed graffiti,
clods of rough-turned earth
thinly sown with seeding grasses;
there's the maze of shrub,
some swings, a scorching slide
and basketball pitch – each thing
stood stranded as if by design
in weed-infested scrub.

3

A few of the trees have plainly died
and parched leaves tell their story –
how in the summer's worst heat
(all civic projects being halted)
even water was denied.

4

That momentary smell at the bridge
over channels reduced to grey slime
is a drain's untreated sewage
dividing the park: one sometime
leftist had stood and split the vote,
let in a minority candidate –
not supported by these afflicted trees.

5

'It's like a film set for "the future",'
as the baby-sitter said.
'What kind?' I asked her, pretty sure
it wouldn't be utopian…
'Something like *Fahrenheit 451*,'
reading my thoughts, she replied.

6

At night, the Vespas' beams
flick across shadowy spaces
as lit globes in crisp leaves
point a way to open waste ground
where, for weeks, the artics park
and our children still not gone
are walked in pushchairs, wide awake,
down towards the Works in Progress
with plenty still left to be done.

7

But then the dusty swags of hose
started to glisten with droplets;
puddles formed round sapling roots
(we'd hear how telephone calls
from citizens to the town hall's
switchboard like dripping taps caused
his change of mind or heart)
and on North Park I paused.

Changing Line

1

At Suzzara, changing line,
you walk across the tracks.
Low platforms are no point of vantage;
flat land which stretches to horizons
marked with solitary villas, some
farmhouse or small village
has excitements still intact –
though not to commuters, I imagine,
those for whom it's home.

Come to a platform's sloped end,
and staring out at furthest
points for the shimmer of approaching trains,
it dawned on me possibilities
couldn't possibly be
in early distances, poplar trees
at intervals across the plain's
cultivated crop and fallow land,
didn't emerge from warming mist
or dewy grass at a field ditch edge.
They had to be imagined.

2

True; but try imagining
the possibles with not a trace
of first mists, hedgerows
diminished by a depth of field
cutting out last skylines,
while the promised sun
draws shapes like a decision
and your slow train presses on –
having got this far.

Yes, and try imagining
where those possibles would be
with not a single thing
to foster them: the pigeons
that, fluttering, change places
in a campanile's apertures
or station clock unmoved by time
or vases of begonias,
their petals flipped by a breeze,
and formed there in the open spaces
possibilities...

3

So –
on a local train with windows open,
over lowlands of the Po,
curtains slapping at a face
flash signals through the empty coach's
mote-filled air; across more points
it lurches, past water tower and sidings.
In fields of rape, grain, cabbage, lucerne,
the stubborn morning sunlight searches
as if for a love's possibilities
and how they illuminate things.

More Aftershocks

1

A lens preserves the ceiling's fall;
below, on hallowed floor,
two monks and two technicians died.
In that corner of the world
now tents are raised through valleys,
Umbrian autumn nights turn cold;
a strained man cools his forehead
with the bared brick of a wall,
its plaster crazed; seismographs read
like heart attacks of blood-splashed stone
'…and we need homes,' as someone said,
'a basilica, we don't need.'

2

Stone on stone, unyielding words
and powdery sunlight fill its nave;
but the part about Francis preaching to birds,
is it intact? did it even survive?

3

What devotion from the volunteers –
to see them not long afterwards
sifting through masonry dust
for bits of surface, down on their knees,
aftershocks coming as strong as the quake,
for tempera fresco in pink, cream or blue
by Giotto and Cimabue –
what patience to restore lost years,
to give us the colouring of the past!

4

'Travelling,' he wrote, 'in the wake of a war
is not the best way of seeing a country…'
Yet the monastery like a citadel
commanded the whole left side of its hill
that autumn, 1944,
when dad in his battledress khaki kit
craned back an itchy neck to catch it –
come in one piece through the war.

5

In plain brown habit, his tonsure bare,
gold halo embossed onto sketchy distance,
arms outstretched, it seems he says,
'No creature lives on bread alone' –
and under the faded leaves they come.
Behind, a fellow monk looks askance
at Francis encouraging birds to praise
the Lord God who made them.

6

I was crossing cut lawn between labs
towards a small alcove of trees,
some trunks sawn flat to form benches,
when the prudent birds took flight
and perched on out-of-reach branches.

St Francis, there was nothing to tell
the sparrows on that autumn day,
nothing of creatures granted souls at last
or many-fold dangers manifested by me;
they knew, and just as well.

Il Trenino

'Papà, cos'è "il futuro"?'

And here you are again
coming out of the tunnel, around a bend,
with sounded bell where beyond painted railings
parents from apparently settled lives
watch children on see-saws, on swings
drop in or out of shadow –
entirely absorbed by whatever they want,
their perpetual present, their *now*.

And here's the toy-town train
coming out of its tunnel, around a bend,
with you once more the engine driver
not noticing us, who've survived to wave
a final hello-goodbye at this end
of another diurnal routine –
set meals, siestas, alarms and excursions
on a line which can't ever be quite the same…

Still, there'll be days, with other people in them,
somebody else who can write their poem,
given, that is, a need or the time –
and here you are again.